If You Give A Lab A Lab:

B⁵arking
Ba⁵⁶d

Again for Ariel & Sam
-S.M.

For Aurora & Celeste
-M.O.

Special Thanks To:
Tosca Miserendino
Stacie Odum
Jack W. Perry
Don Loudon
Ron Riffle
Travis Bundy
Shawn Gates
Beverly Miserendino

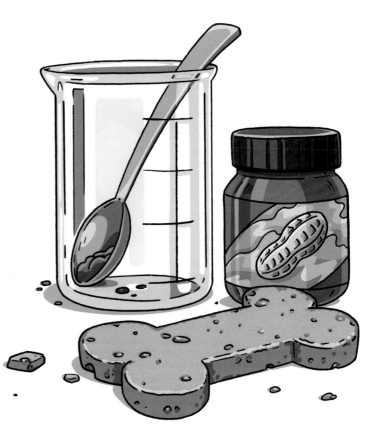

If You Give A Lab A Lab

B⁵arking

Bad⁵⁶

Written By Sam Miserendino
Illustrated By Mike Odum

Skyhorse Publishing, Inc.

Leaves Of Grass

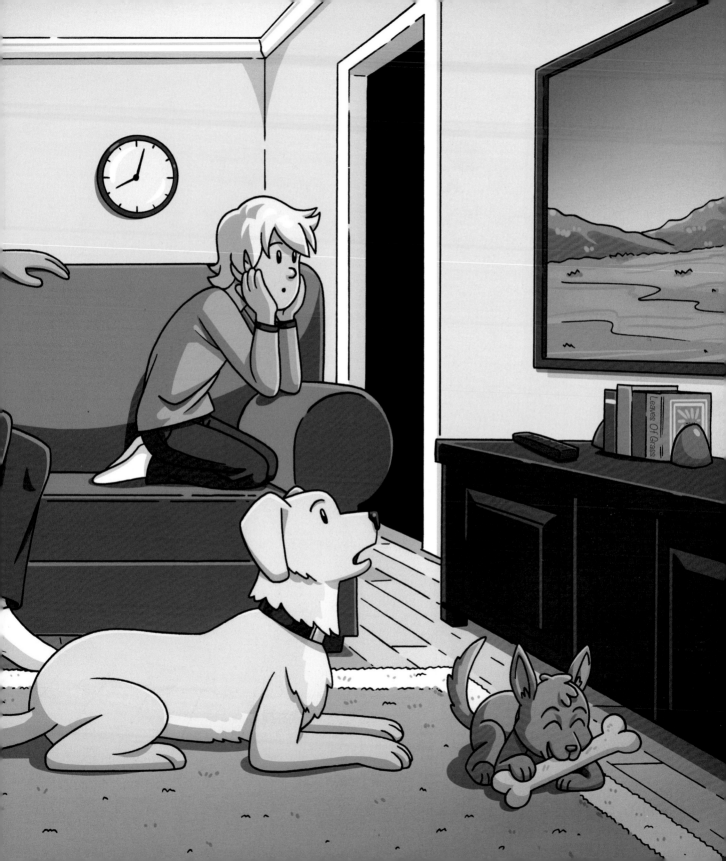

ZZZ

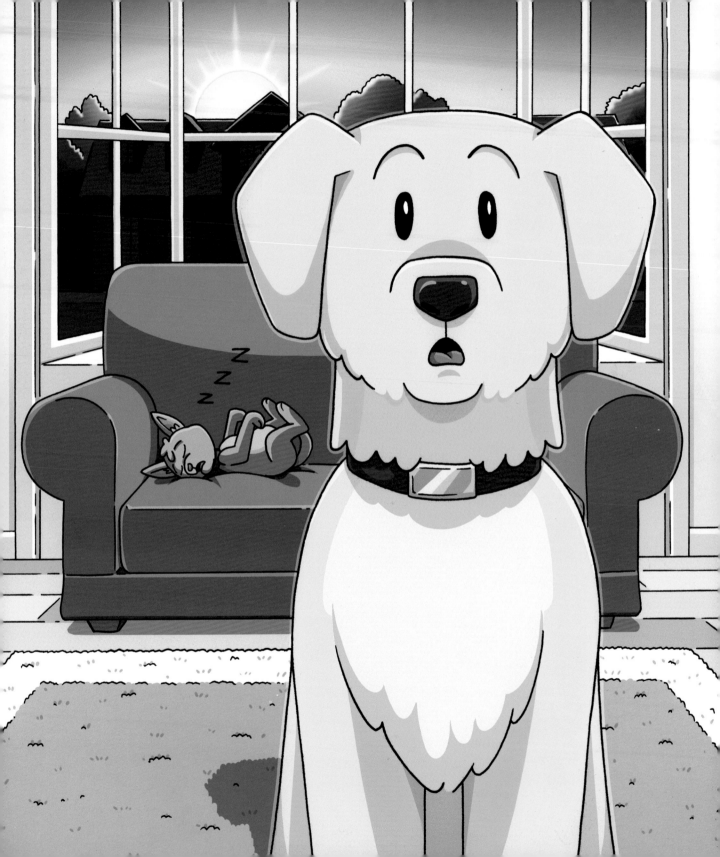

CHEMISTRY
FOR KIDS

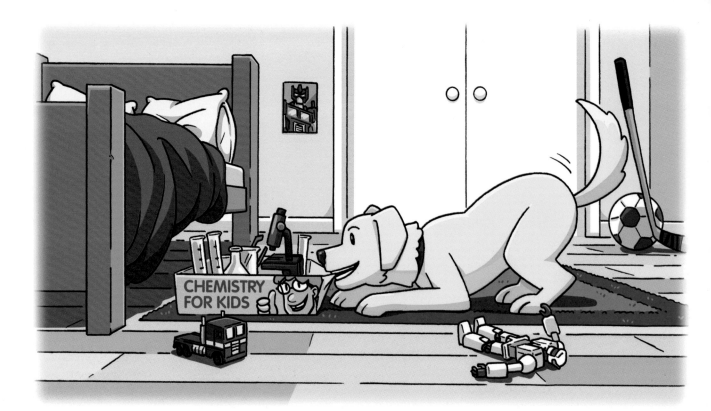

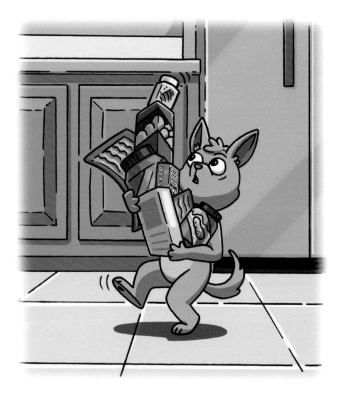

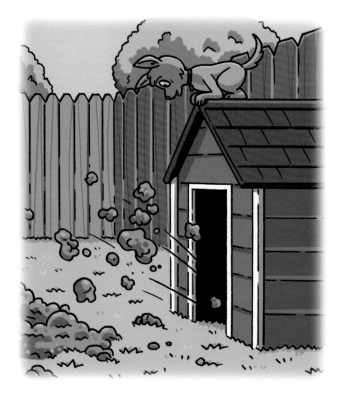

CHEMISTRY
FOR KIDS
CHEMISTRY
FOR KIDS
COLD-B-GONE
COLD-B-GONE

If you give a lab
a lab…

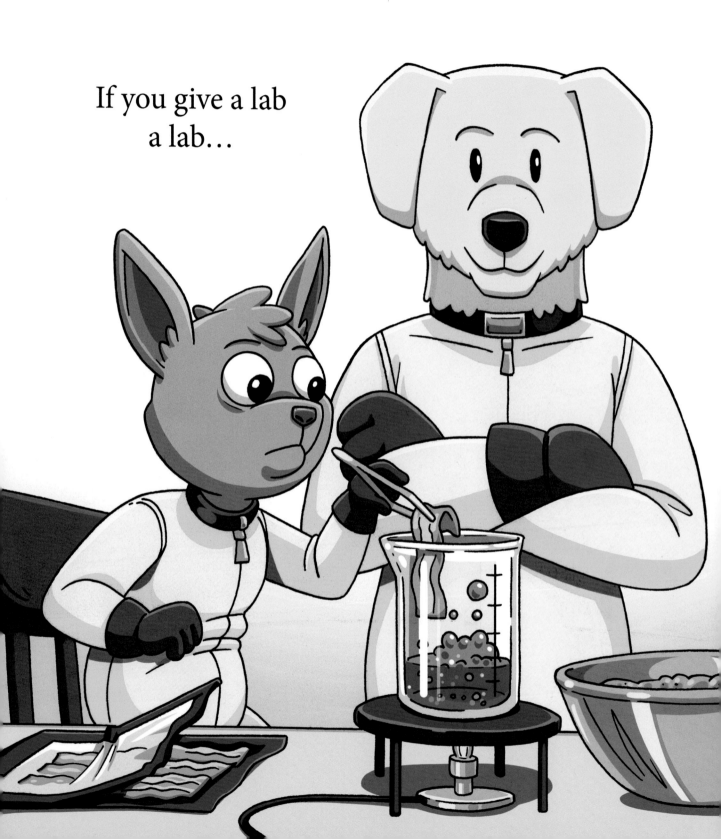

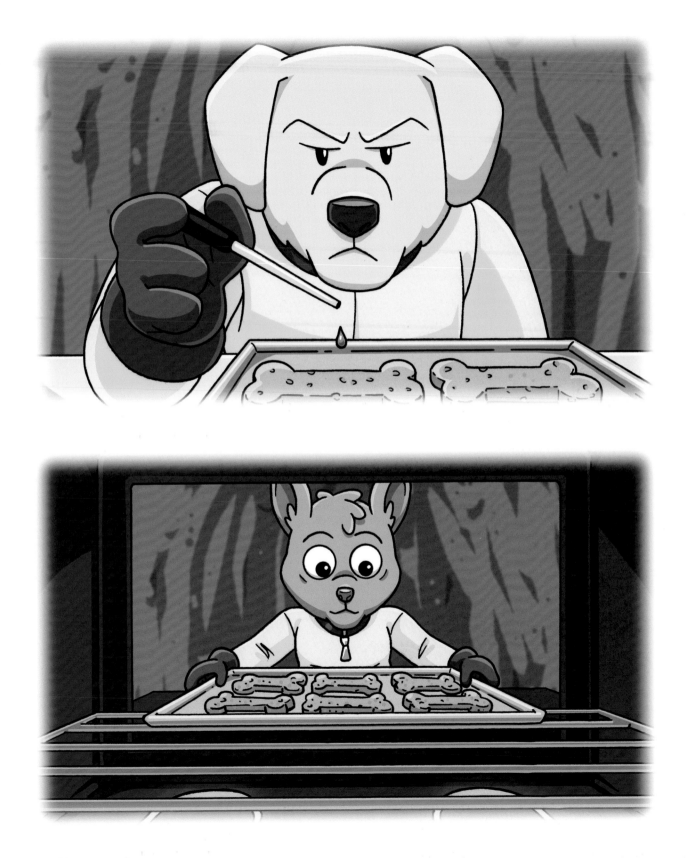

he'll make the most amazing
dog treats ever!

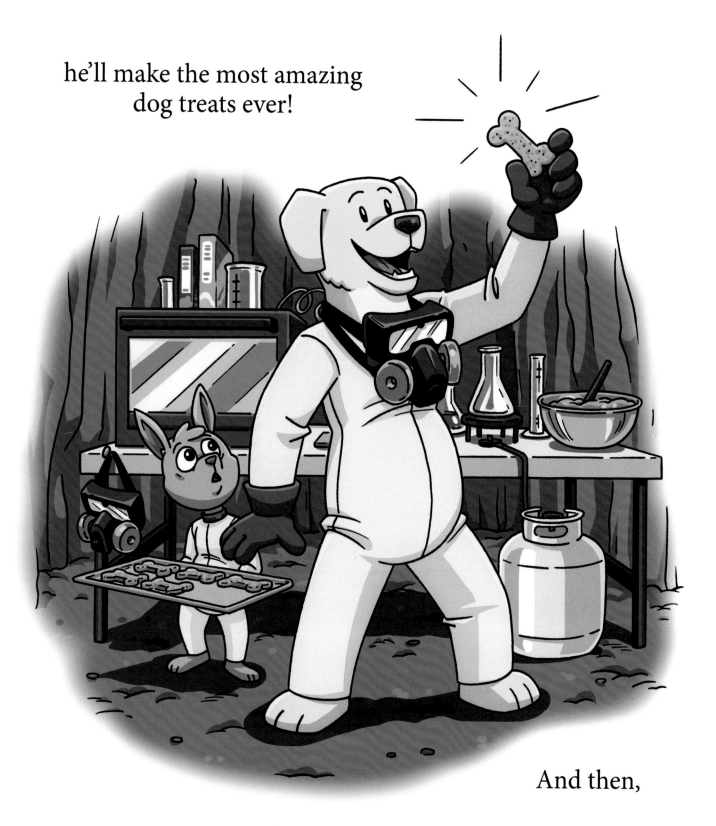

And then,

he'll share them with
his friends...

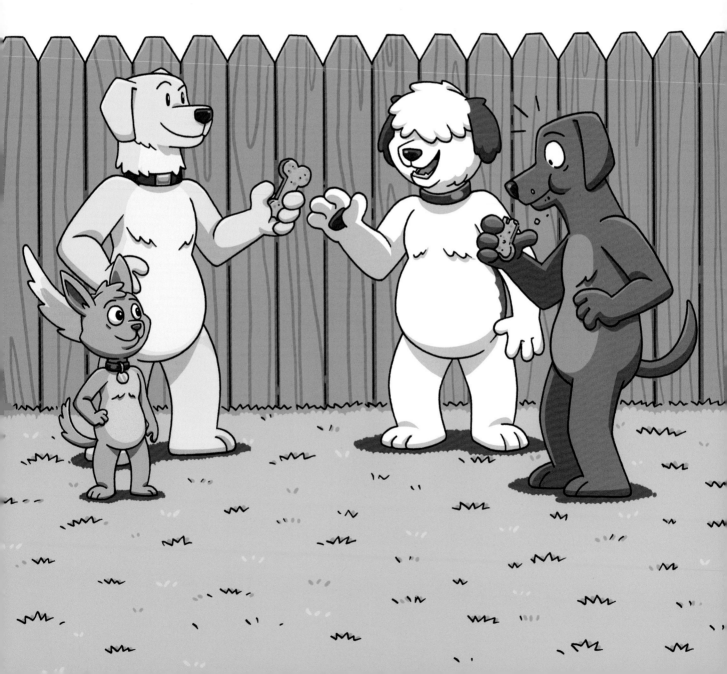

who will tell their friends...

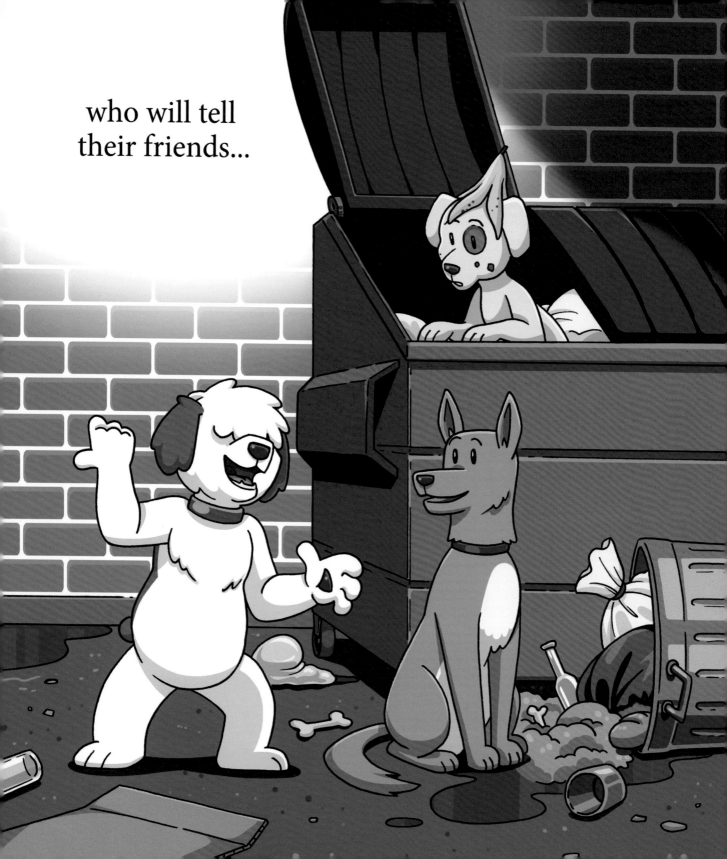

who will tell their friends...

And soon,

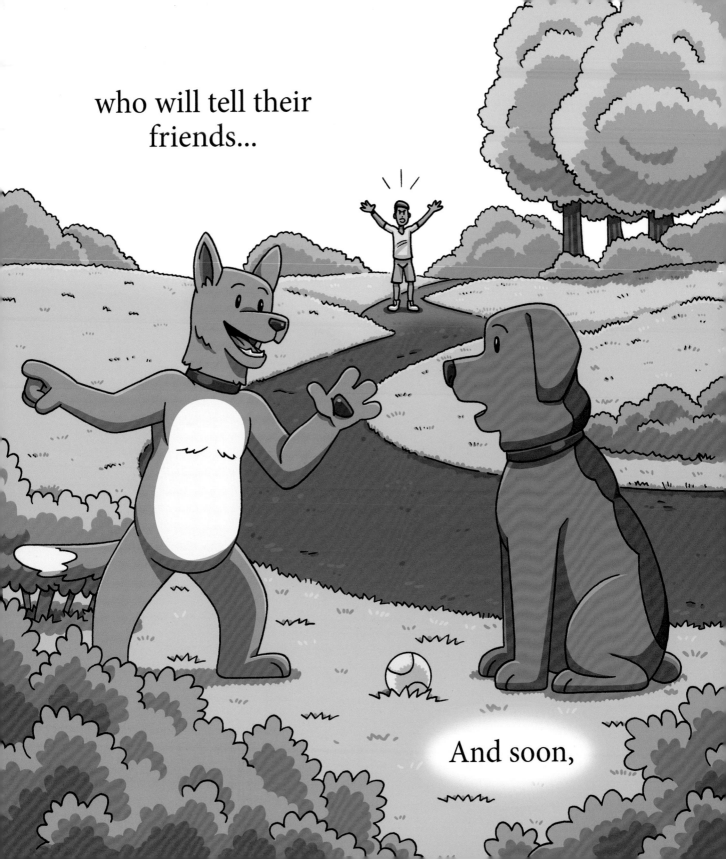

every dog in the neighborhood will want to try his incredible blue biscuits...

Again...

And again...

And again,
until...

his humans come home.

When he greets them, he'll give them the cutest, sweetest lab-look ever, and they won't suspect a thing.

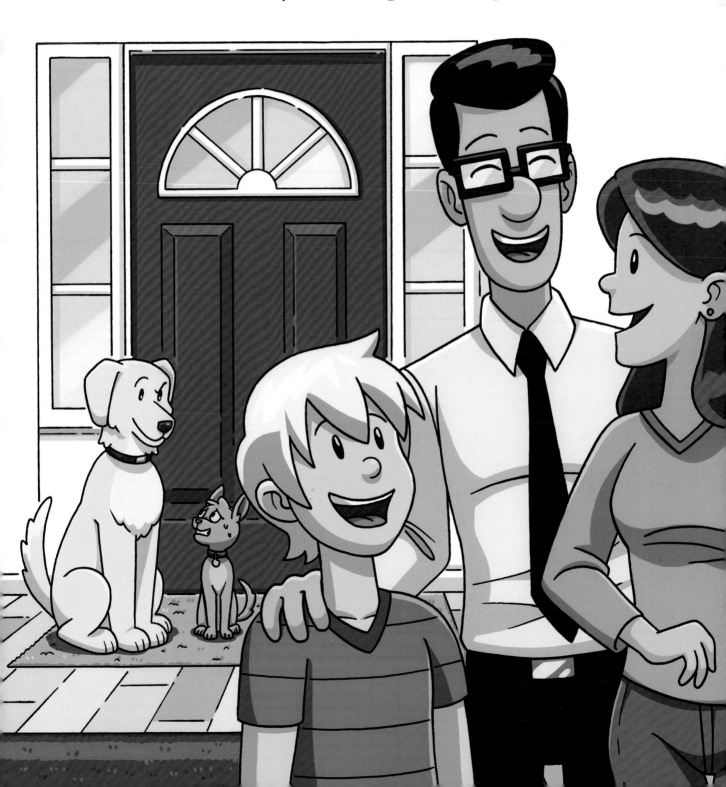

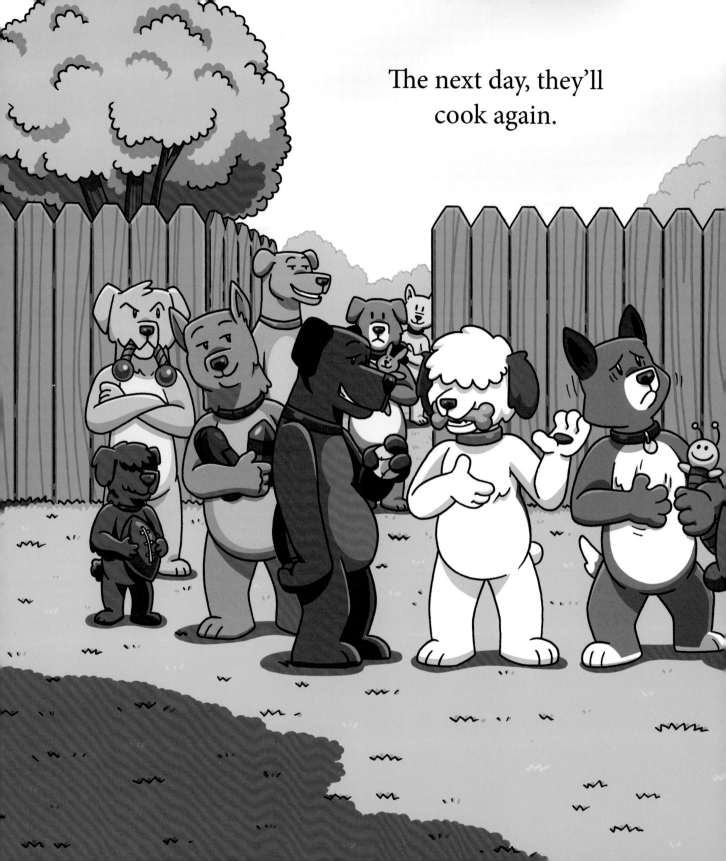

The next day, they'll cook again.

By the end of the
day, they'll have so many
chew toys...

they won't know
what to do.

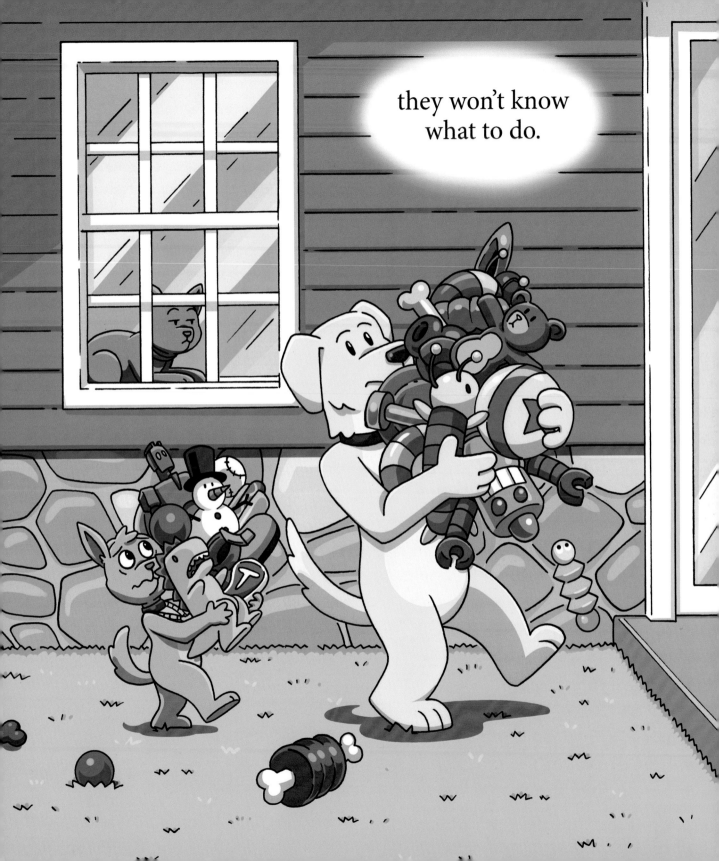

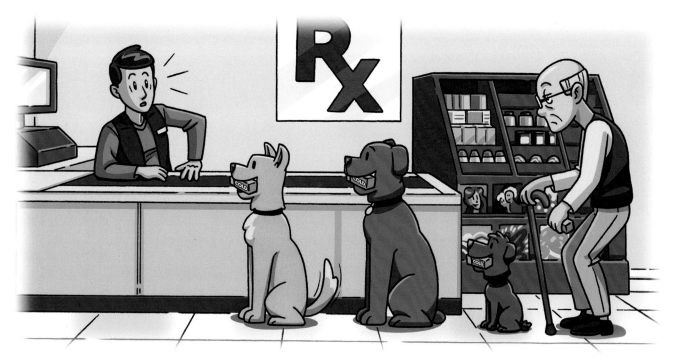

Meanwhile, people are starting to
notice that the dogs in the neighborhood
are acting strange...

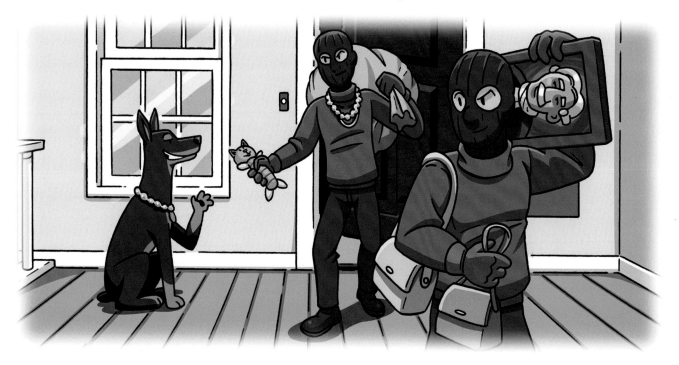

really, really strange.

CLOSED
Talbott's
Pet Palace
GOODFIN

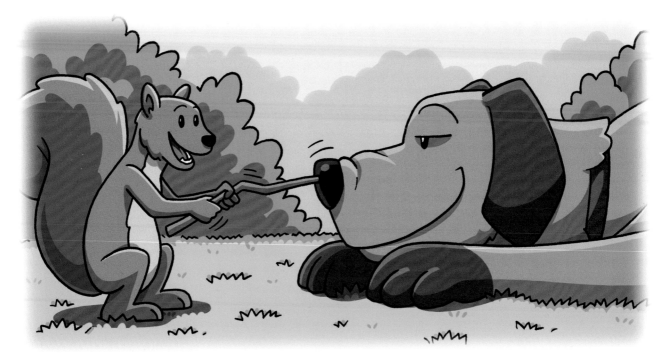

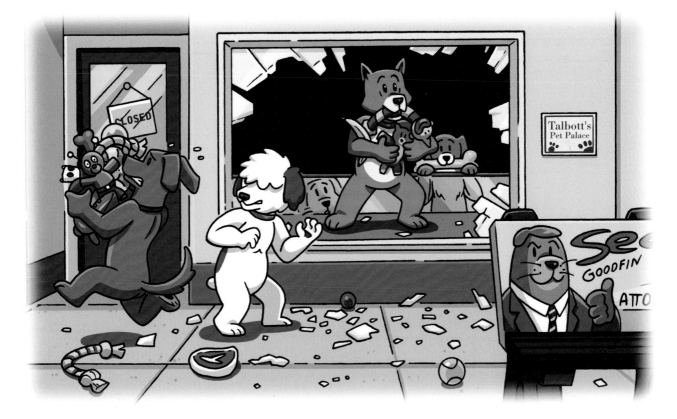

Back at home...

Rob Boss

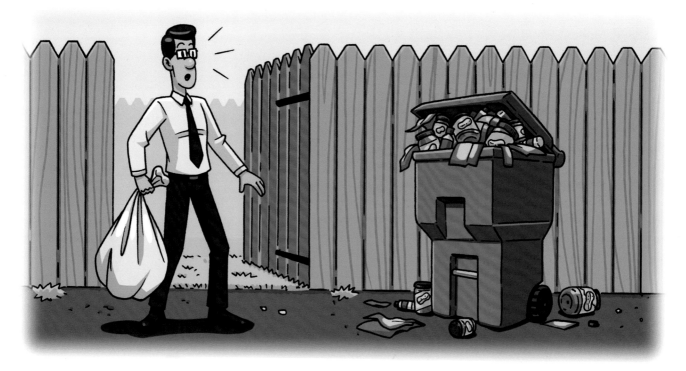

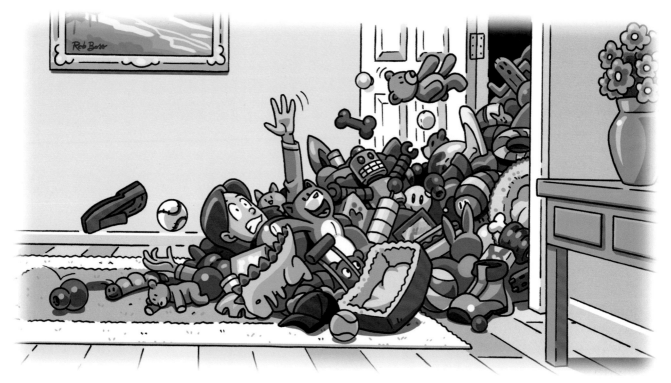

the questions begin
to swirl.

They'll ask him
where all the chew toys
came from,

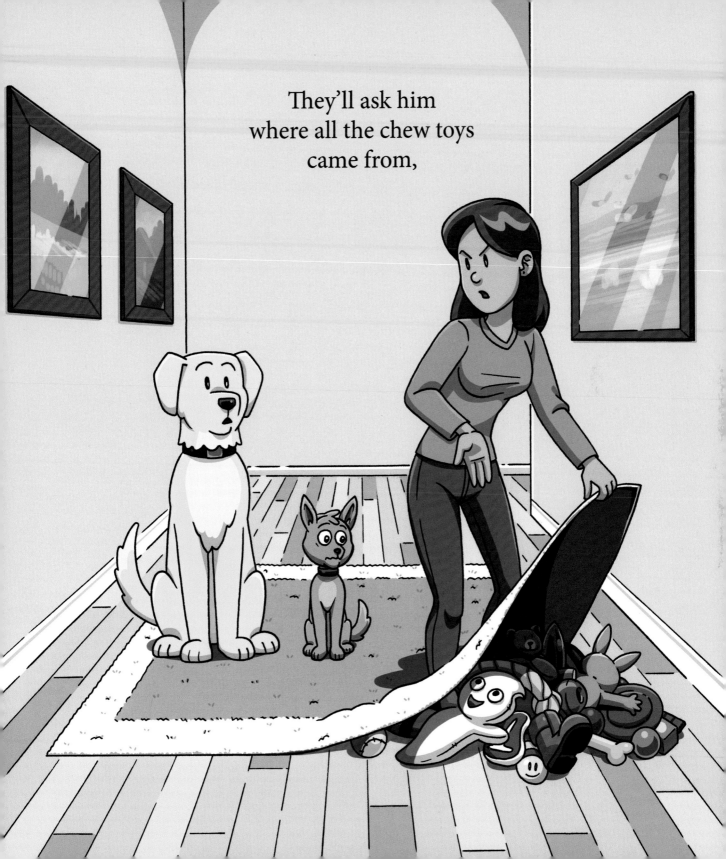

and what happened to
all of that food.

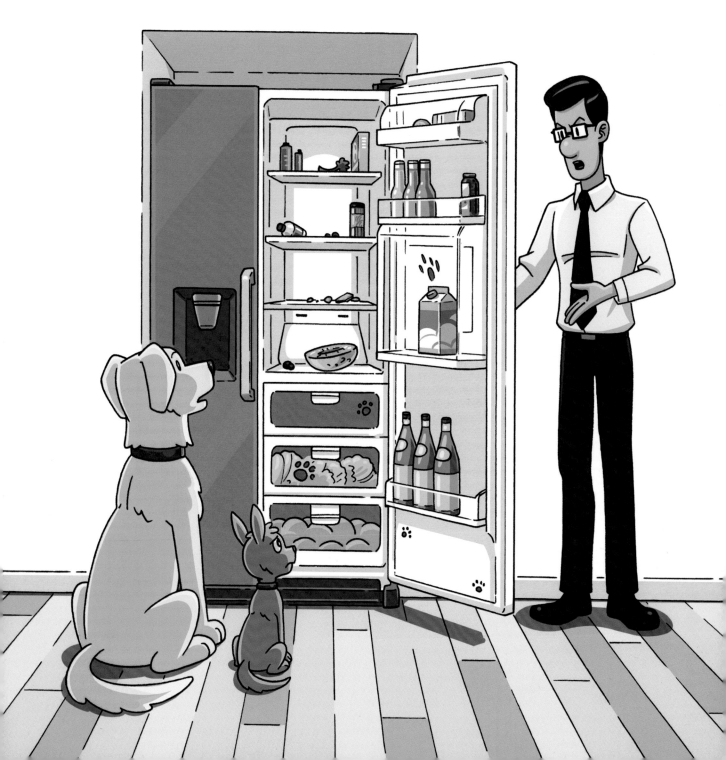

But most of all, they'll want to know why
there are so many dogs in the yard.

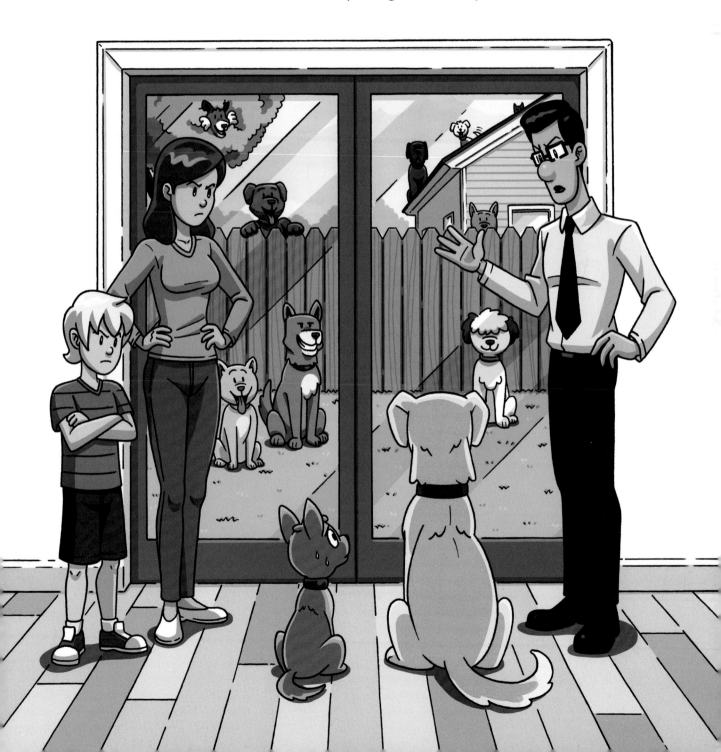

When he tells them it's
all the cat's fault,

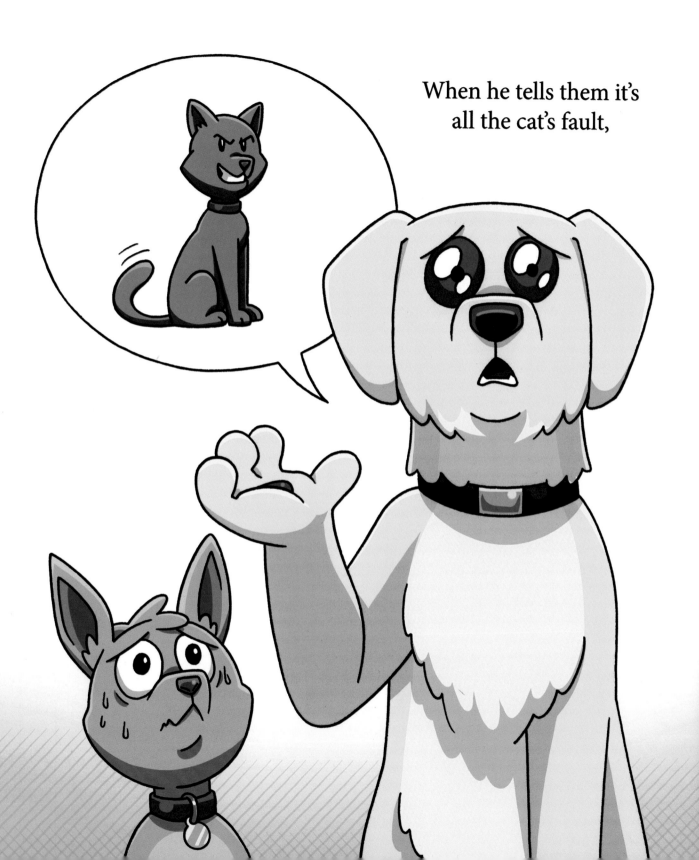

they will remember all of the bad
things the cat has done,

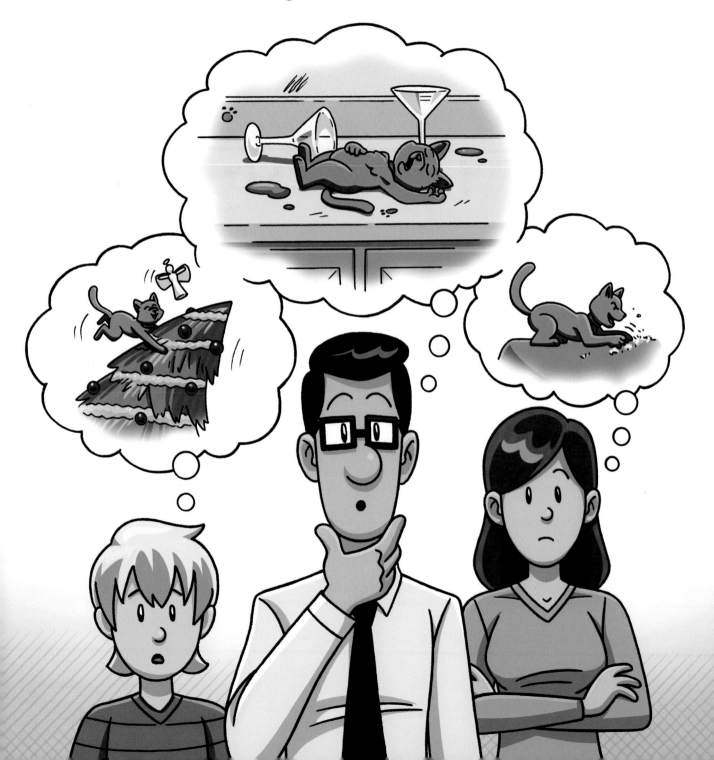

and his humans will believe him.

After such a close call, he'll decide it's not safe to bring the dogs to the treats, so...

they'll bring the treats to the dogs.

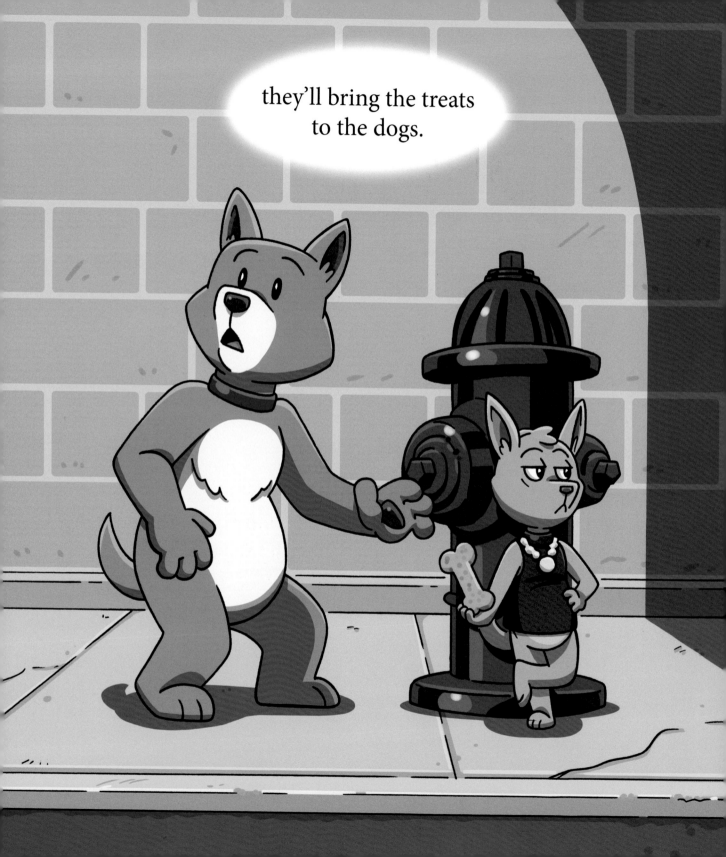

And they will sell...

THE GROOM ROOM

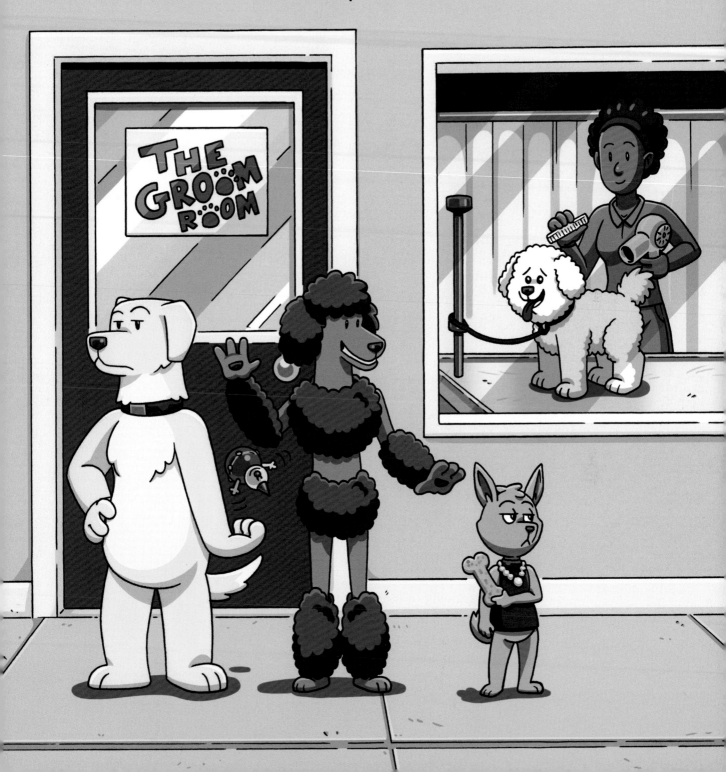

And sell...

PIECES
Dr. Robert

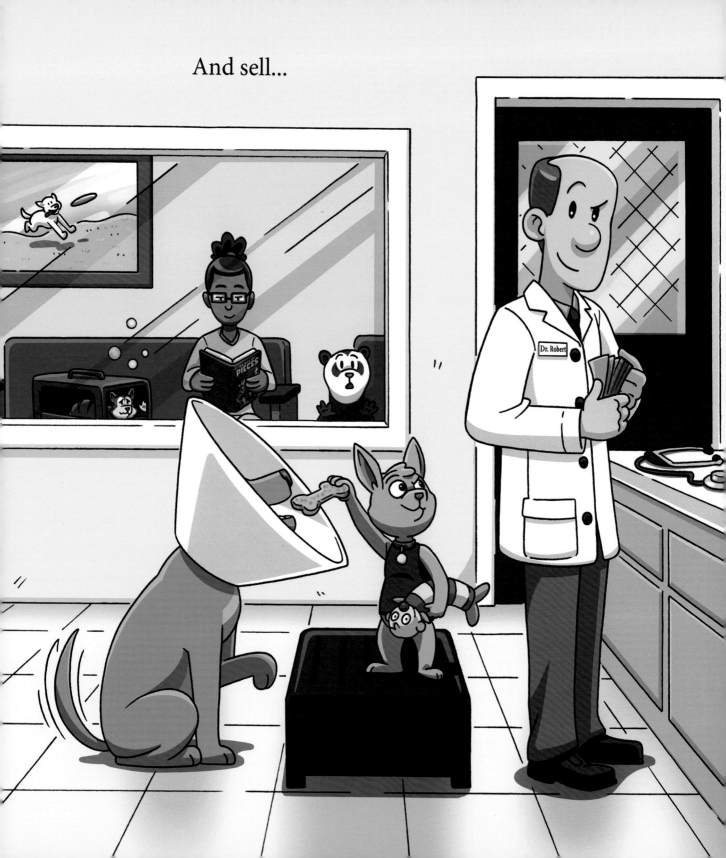

And sell...
Until...

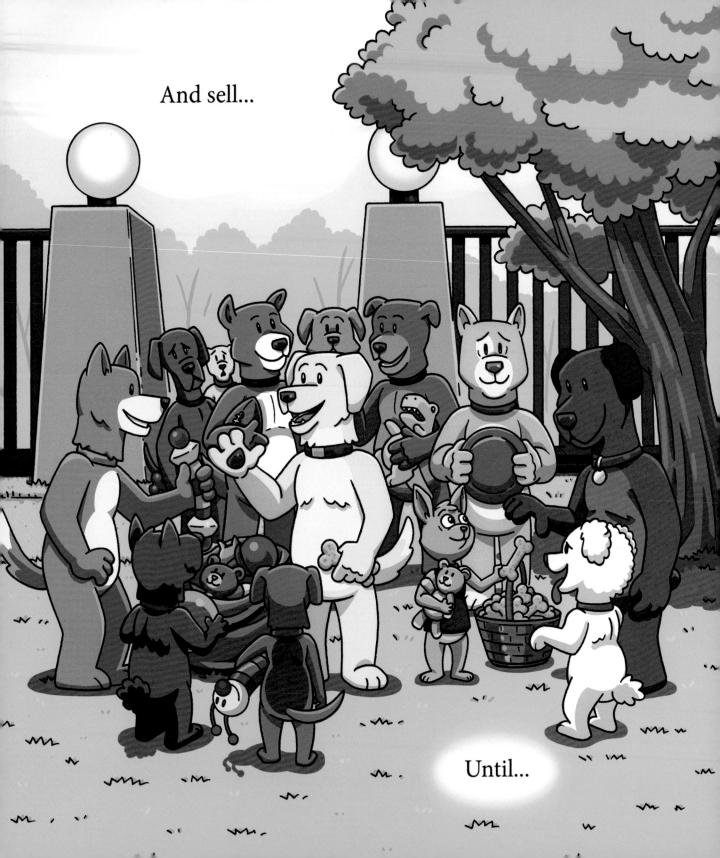

they sell in the territory
of another dog...

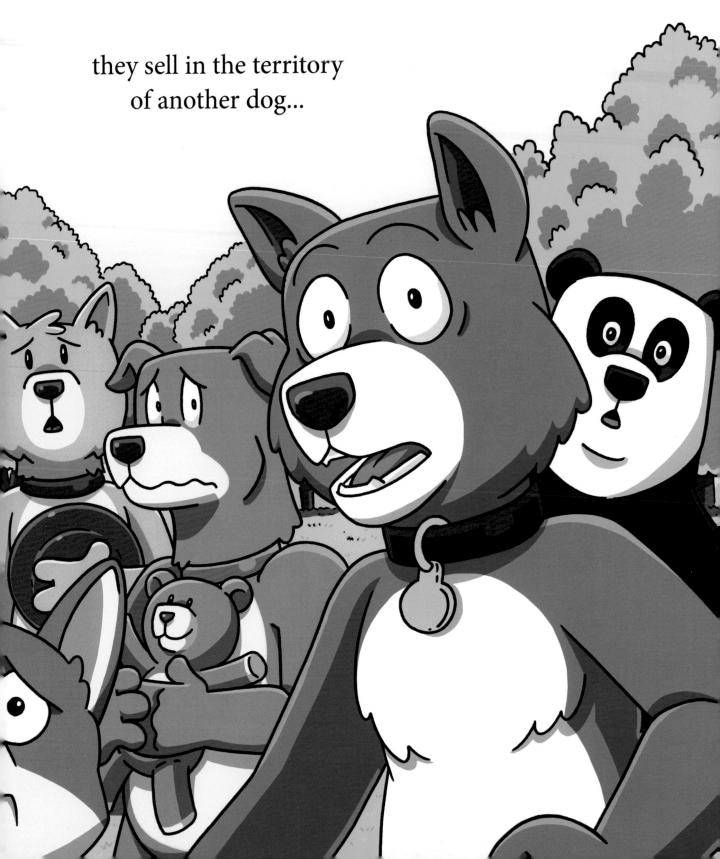

A *very* mean dog,

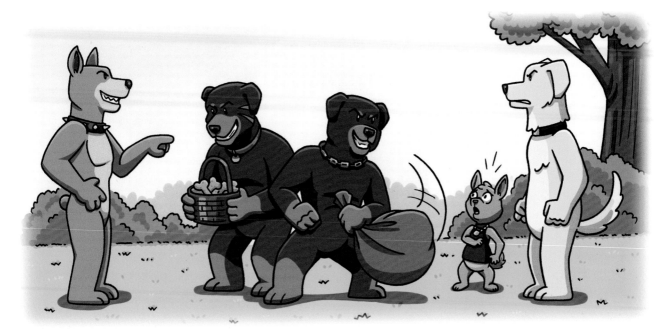

who will tell them that from now on their treats are
his treats, and their chew toys are his chew toys.

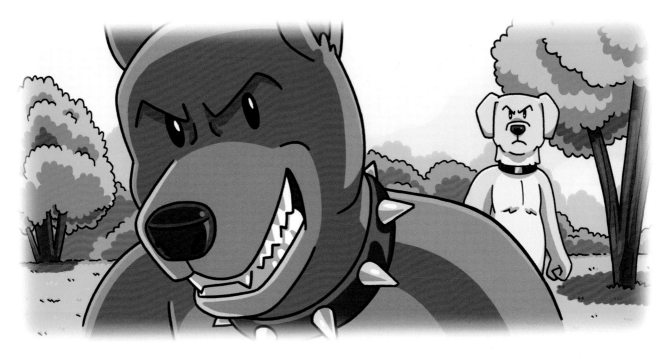

And just to make absolutely sure they understand,

the very mean dog will
send them a message.

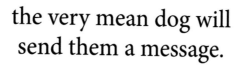

After that,

he'll add a few touches
to his doghouse.

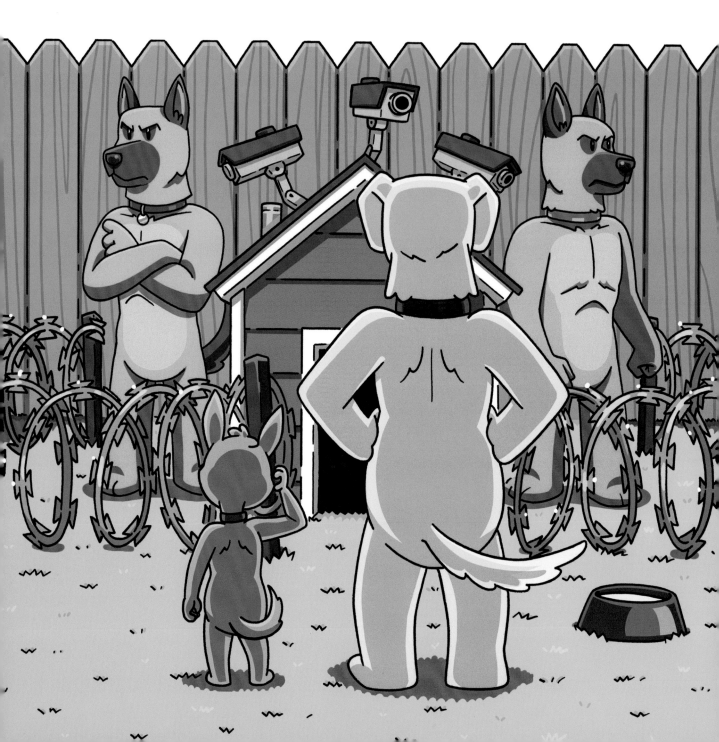

When his human asks him about the cameras,
the fence, and the guard dogs,

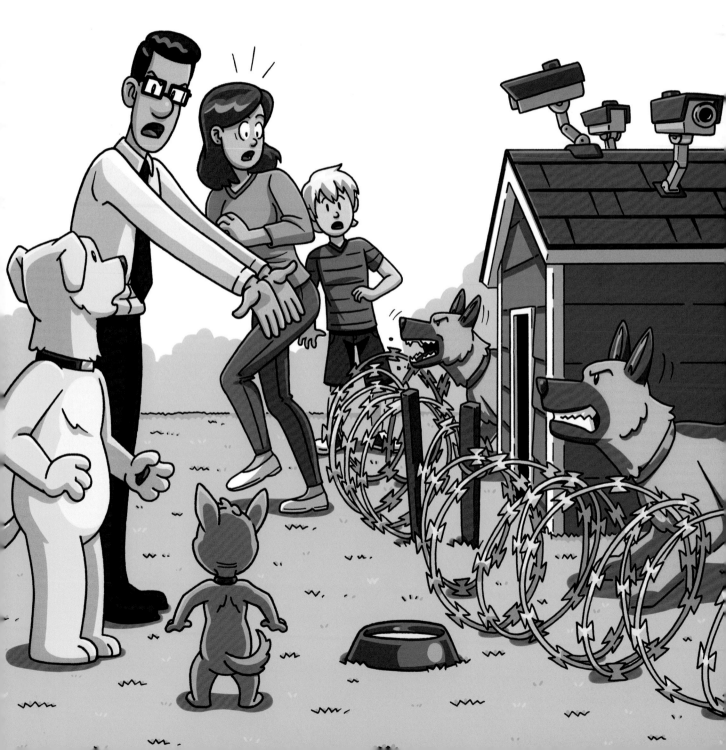

he'll tell him it's a dog-eat-dog world,
and you can't be too careful.

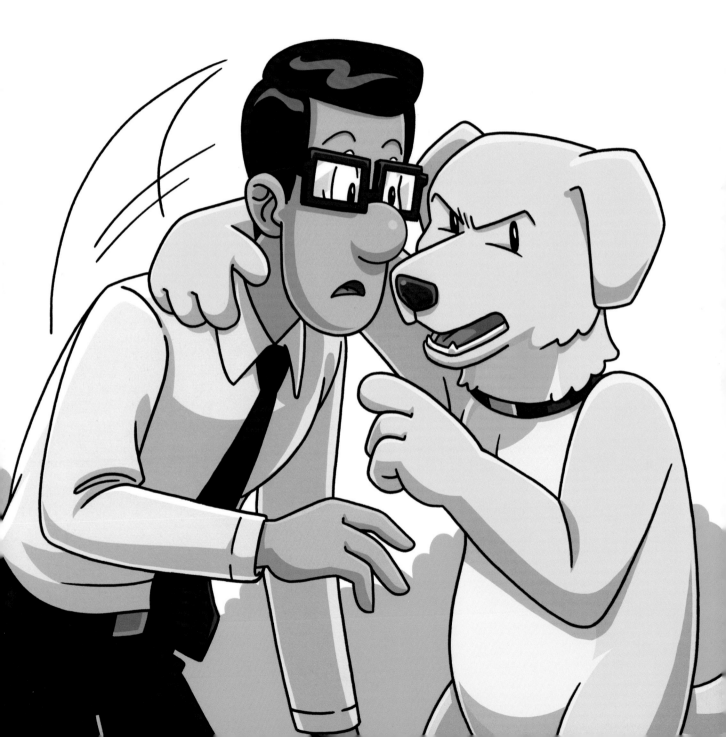

That night, he'll make a treat for the very mean dog…

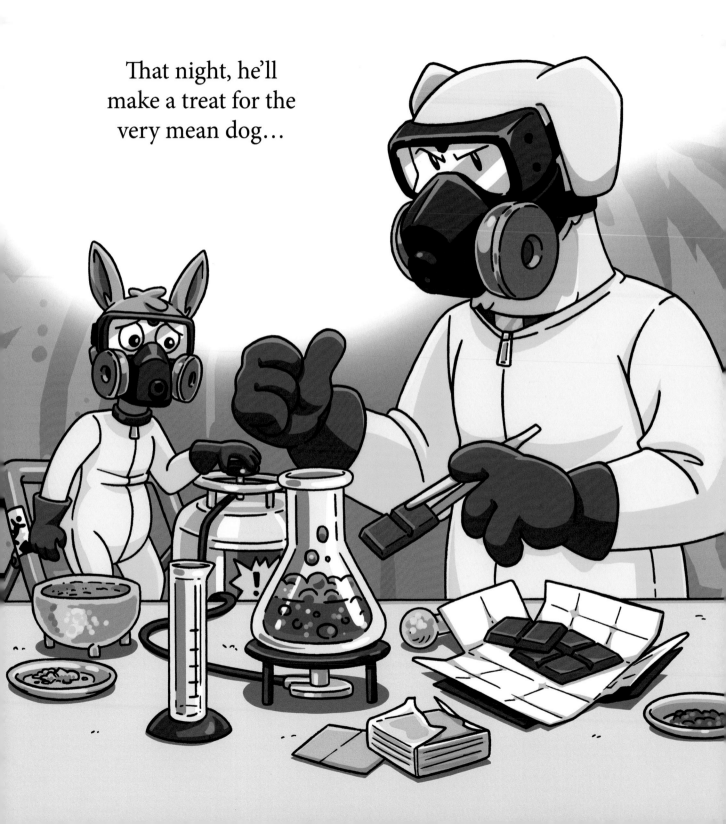

an extra-special treat…

With his rival out
of the way,

HAVE YOU SEEN ME?
ANSWERS TO "MR. CUDDLES"
HAVE YOU SEEN ME?

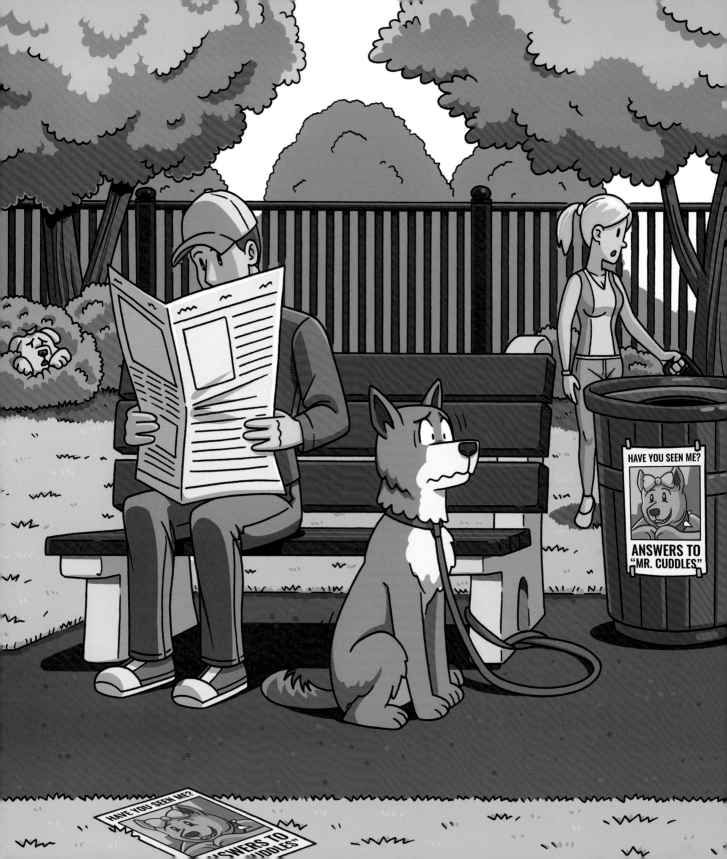

everyone will know
he's the top dog.

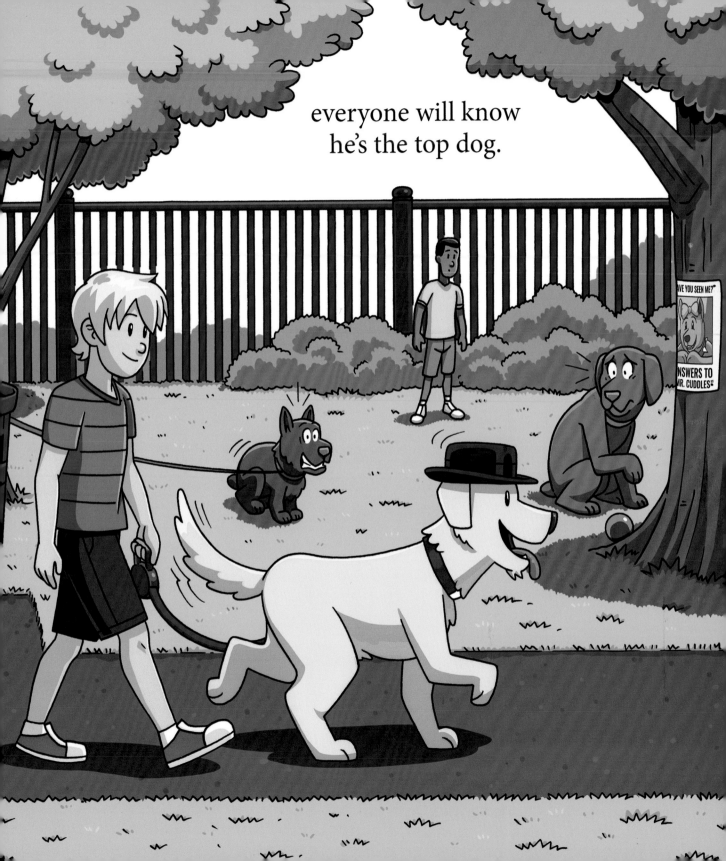

And his empire will
grow and grow

FANCY
PUP

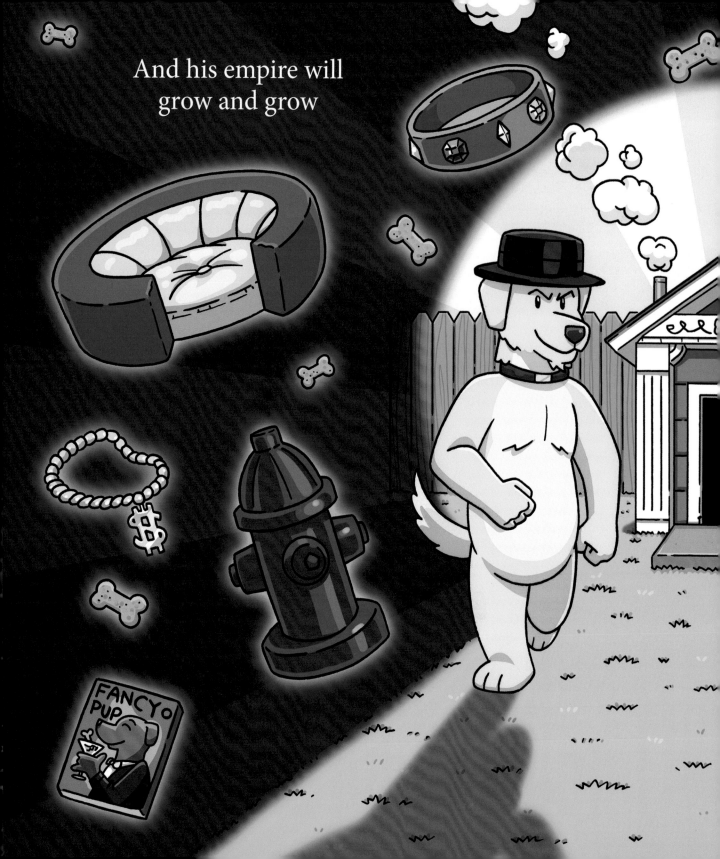

KONGO
BOSS DOG
JUMBO

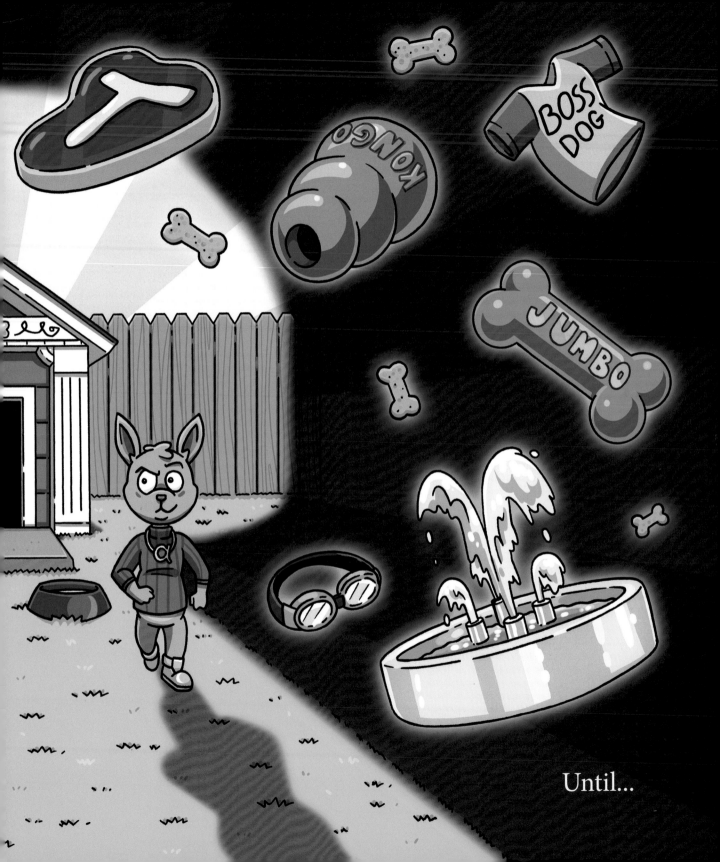

Until...

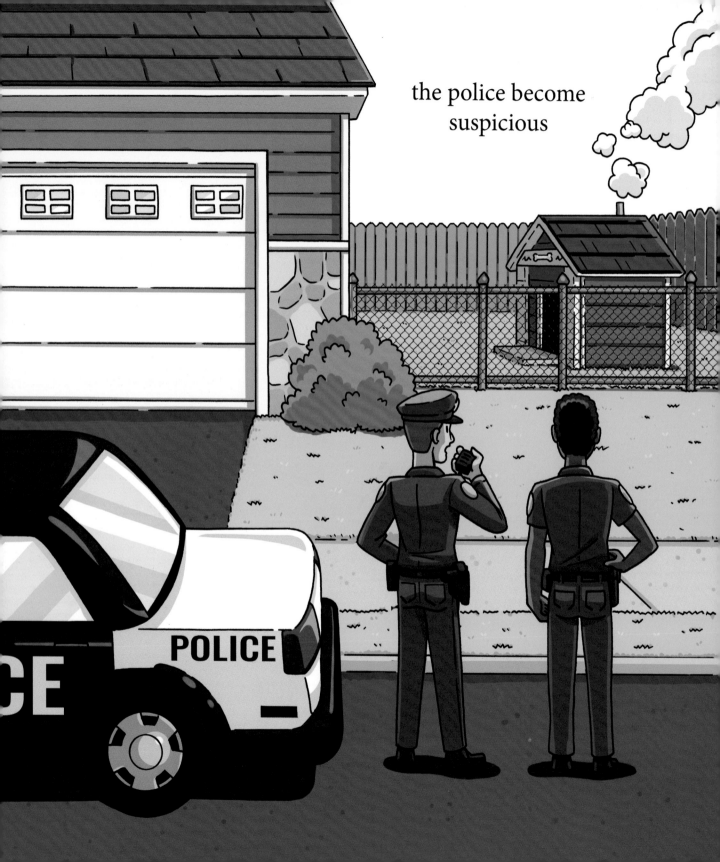

the police become
suspicious

and begin offering belly rubs for information.

OPTIMAL
BELLY RUBS
GOOD
GREAT

And once the dogs start speaking,

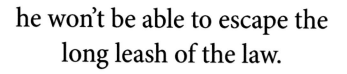

he won't be able to escape the
long leash of the law.

POLICE
POLICE
POLICE
POLICE
POLICE
POLICE

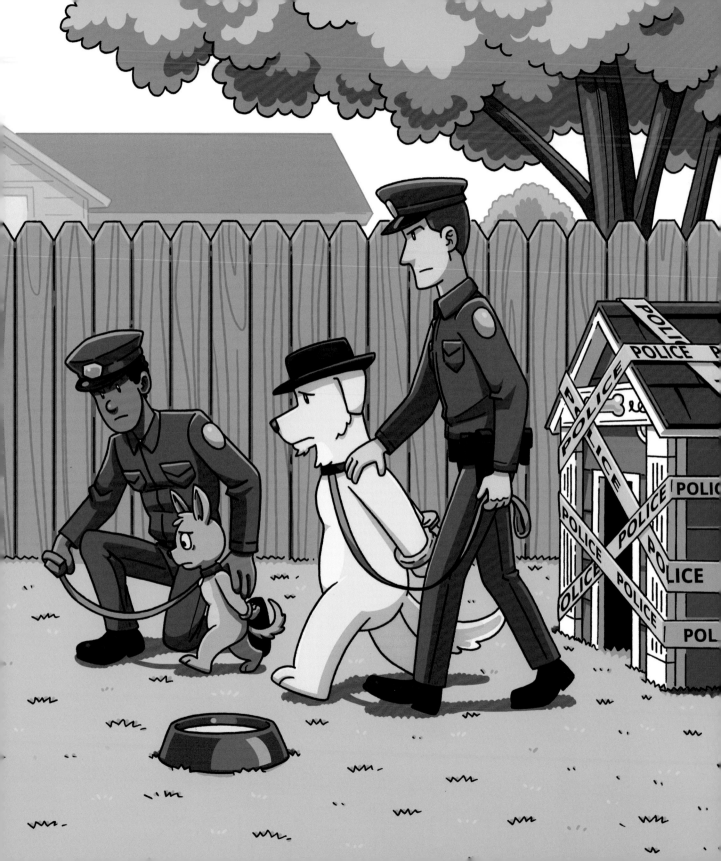

The judge will find him guilty
of being a very bad boy

S.Goodfin

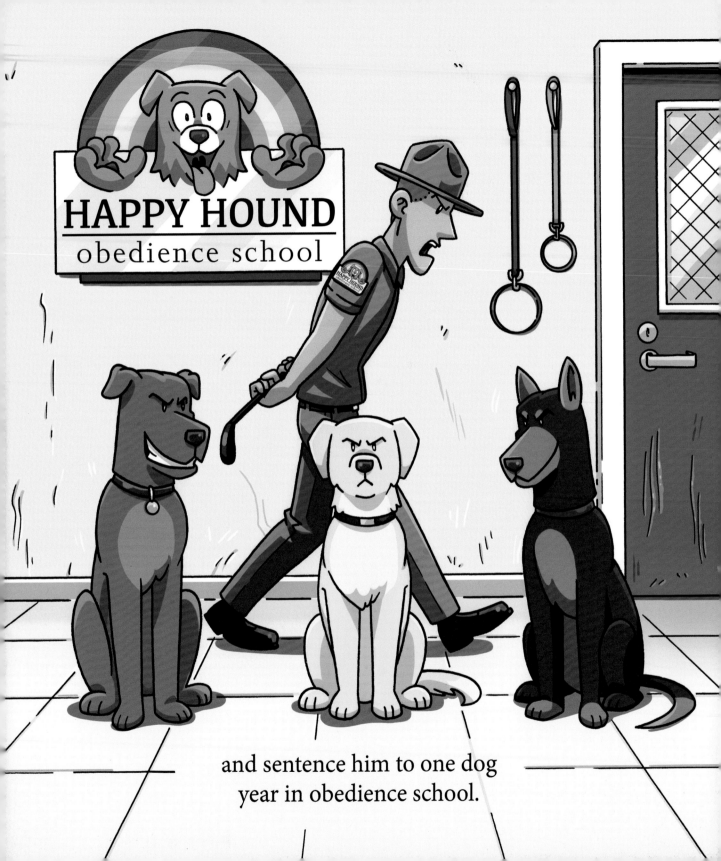

and sentence him to one dog
year in obedience school.

When he graduates, he'll swear he'll never, ever make another special treat again.

But when he thinks about the power and the toys...all those wonderful, chewy, squeaky toys...

He will!

The End

Skyhorse Publishing books may be purchased in bulk at special discounts for sales promotion, corporate gifts, fund-raising, or educational purposes. Special editions can also be created to specifications. For details, contact the Special Sales Department, Skyhorse Publishing, 307 West 36th Street, 11th Floor, New York, NY 10018 or info@skyhorsepublishing.com.

Skyhorse® and Skyhorse Publishing® are registered trademarks of Skyhorse Publishing, Inc.®, a Delaware corporation.

Visit our website at www.skyhorsepublishing.com.

10 9 8 7 6 5 4 3 2 1

Library of Congress Cataloging-in-Publication Data is available on file

Cover and interior artwork by Mike Odum

Print ISBN: 978-1-5107-7252-6
E-book ISBN: 978-1-5107-7359-2

Printed in China